TRAVIS

Jorjan Jane

Author's Tranquility Press
ATLANTA, GEORGIA

Jorjan Jane/Author's Tranquility Press
3900 N Commerce Dr. Suite 300 #1255
Atlanta, GA 30344, USA
www.authorstranquilitypress.com

Ordering Information:
Quantity sales. Special discounts are available on quantity purchases by corporations, associations, and others. For details, contact the "Special Sales Department" at the address above.

Travis /Jorjan Jane
Hardback: 978-1-964810-74-4
Paperback: 978-1-964810-75-1
eBook: 978-1-964810-24-9

Contents

Dear *Travis*,

Happy Birthday! I have written a short story about you for your 45th birthday. I did the same for your brother, Gregg, when he turned 45 years old.

I have written about some of the memorable things that occurred when dating your Dad. I have also included tales of your youth and insights of your future. We all see life a bit differently, so each saga has its own personal twist.

Of course, it is slanted by a mother's point of view and my unconditional love. Again, Happy Birthday, Son.

Love,
Mom

Chapter 1

Travis, I met your Dad on the steps of the apartment building on Van Patton Street in Las Vegas. He was going to work at the test site early in the morning and I was coming home from work at the Desert Inn, late at night. He was too shy to say anything but "hi," so he paid the landlord fifty dollars to properly introduce us. She did and the rest is history.

Everyone called him Red because he had bright red hair. He said that red hair ran in the family. He had two redheaded brothers and two sisters with auburn hair.

Travis, your Dad mustered up enough nerve to ask me out, but I had to decline, because I already had a date. He looked so dejected, but then he said, "If you change your mind just let me know."

He only lived two apartments down from me. I guess it was fate that my date couldn't find my apartment. Then again, he could have stood me up. I walked over to Red's door and knocked. "I have reconsidered and would be happy to go out with you, if the offer still stands," I said. He beamed and nodded his head, "yes."

When I walked back to lock my apartment door, I saw that the number six on my door had the top nail out. It slipped down and now looked like a nine. How did that happen? I wondered. Then I was thankful that my date couldn't find my apartment because anyone who couldn't figure that between apartments five and seven was six wasn't too swift. I didn't need to be dating someone like that.

Our date was a disaster. We went to the Hilltop Restaurant for dinner. Steak was the house specialty, but there were a lot of unusual items on the menu like frog legs. After Red ordered, he saw the Teamsters union boss leaving the restaurant. He followed him to the parking lot, and they had a heated argument that almost came to blows. There was a lot of finger pointing and head shaking. I watched them from the window where I was sitting. Our meal arrived but he didn't come inside. I waited and waited then finally ate. He came in just to pay the bill, and we left. I surmised they were arguing over a union issue at the Test Site, but the dispute left Red upset all evening, and probably hungry as well.

During our conversation, I asked, "What did you do before driving a truck at the test site?"

He said, "I was a roughneck."

"Okay," I said, "other than your behavior, what type of work did you do?"

He said again, "I was a roughneck."

"You mean that's a job? Is it like being a bouncer in a bar?

"No," he said.

"Well, tell me what a roughneck does, I asked curiously."

"A roughneck works in the oil fields on a drilling rig as a common laborer doing all the dirty work. It's a job nobody wants, but you have to start at the bottom and work your way up."

"What was the next step up?" I inquired.

"A swamper," he said. "That is a trucker's helper and I did that for a while. I finally worked my way up to a truck driver. Fortunately, I had an excellent trucker teach me to drive. There wasn't anything that man couldn't do with a truck. He could change gears so smoothly. You never felt the shift from one gear to the next. I didn't realize how good he was, until I had ridden with a few other drivers. There was no comparison. He was the best."

He said, "I had the opportunity to move a drilling rig to the Nevada Test Site in 1960, and after seeing Las Vegas, I just knew that this was the town for me. I had never seen so many lights in my life. We didn't have electricity at home when I grew up, so it was mind boggling."

When I saw Red again on the steps of the apartment building, I asked, "Could I give your telephone number at my work place in case of an emergency?"

"Sure," he said, "I have no problem with that." I didn't have a phone; I simply couldn't afford the deposit. I was a single Mom with a son nearly three years old. I was very careful about spending needlessly. I knew that my biggest expense was rent followed by food and babysitters. The apartment manager's daughter usually watched Gregg for me. She was a responsible teenager. I was fortunate to have a baby sitter living so close.

The first time I went to Red's apartment to use his phone, he ran over and opened the curtains, and left the door open with the air conditioner running. I closed the door, but he ran over and opened it again. Oh, whatever. I couldn't figure that out. A year after we were married, I asked, "Why did you do that?"

He said, "Because my mother warned me about the fast women in Las Vegas. She pleaded with me to come home before it was too late. She stressed the fact that I was living in a sinful city."

I was still in shock thinking he was scared of me. Then he told me he had some money hidden in his sock drawer.

"I was afraid that somehow you were going to snooker me out it by making some smooth moves to distract me, or at the least, cloud my judgment."

I nearly hit him, but instead shook my head in disbelief. "For heaven sakes, did you think I was a hooker?"

"I didn't know what you were, so I had to be careful."

But the next time we met was a shocker. He asked, "Would you like to go to Los Angeles for breakfast?"

I said, "How are we going to do that, and get back to Las Vegas in time for me to go to work at seven p.m.?"

"Oh, we will fly there," he said, nonchalantly.

"But don't we have to make prior arrangements, by getting the airline tickets?"

"No, I have my own plane."

"Wow!" I said, surprised at what I just heard. "Okay, I'll go." I answered, in a state of excitement.

The next day, a friend told Red of a great restaurant at the airport at Site Six which was later renamed Lake Havasu Airport, so we ended up flying there for breakfast, and had a wonderful time. There was a lot less air traffic than Los Angeles.

Red lived high on the hog. He had a beautiful, new, burgundy Grand Prix, Pontiac. He had an airplane and also paid for hangar space in which to park the Cessna. He enjoyed good food and drink. So knowing that he was from Oklahoma, I figured that he also had oil wells, so I bluntly told him that I was going to marry him for his money.

When we decided to get married, we went to the court house to get our marriage license. It was on a Thursday, the day before payday. The license cost two dollars, and he only had one dollar. I pitched in the other buck and told myself that it wasn't too late to back out. He evidently lived from payday to payday. This was not a good sign. He said that with me paying for half of the marriage license showed that he was not a chauvinist. He would allow me to pay half just to prove it. This way I had a stake in our future. He talked slow with his Oklahoma drawl, but boy, he could think fast.

He had a stuttering problem which he eventually overcame. That is until he had a few drinks. Then the speech problems came back, and a more pronounced Okie accent.

Chapter 2

Travis, before you were even born you were with me through all my ups and downs. I say that because in 1964, you (just a tiny embryo), and I flew on a piano wire, up high near the ceiling of the stage. I was one of two butterflies dancing at the Desert Inn. There was a distinct difference between the two butterflies. I was the pregnant one. We flew above the stage with strobe lights flashing to catch the brilliant colors of our psychedelic wings.

To fly fulfilled one of my delightful childhood dreams, but I worried that the tight harness might harm you. It fits like a cinched corset. There were double straps that crossed between the legs and would pinch badly. The stagehands controlled our accent and decent, so it was wise to stay on the good side of them. Whenever they didn't pull slowly and evenly as we took flight, we would start twisting. The slightest bounce could cause us to turn in the air unable to face the audience. No matter how we flapped our wings we were completely helpless. Any jerk would send off a chain reaction causing excruciating pain when the crotch straps overlapped. At this point, we would invariably start the uncontrollable rotation, twelve feet above the stage. We were truly at the mercy of the stage hands. There was no way a male could wear that harness. He would end up a eunuch with a high squeaky voice.

One night the stagehand operating my wire and rope was evidently drunk. He let go of the rope thinking I had landed, but I was still four feet off the floor. Unexpectedly, I came down abruptly with a thud. That was my last flight; I didn't want to take any more chances with your health and well-being, after all, I was now four months pregnant. The line captain took my place, so I could avoid any injuries. I hope that your fear of heights doesn't have anything to do with that pre-birth experience.

Before leaving the show, the dancers gave me a baby shower. My friend, Marliss, was very happy and full of joy over my pregnancy. I never saw anyone so elated. It made me feel good. I vowed that I would follow her example, by showing the same excitement, whenever I heard someone was expecting a baby —no matter the circumstances. Marliss had been hit by a car in Berlin at age fifteen. She had internal injuries leaving her unable to bear children. That was such a shame, because she would have been a wonderful mom.

Your Dad and I didn't want to waste any more money paying rent. We preferred our money going toward a mortgage payment on a home. After looking in various areas of town, we settled on a house on Falcon Lane, with a huge back yard. Now, I had a house to get in order before you were born.

The street should have been renamed "Motherhood Lane." There were four of us expecting within a few months of each other. Later five more families moved in the neighborhood having children your age. From May to August there were weekly birthday parties. It was Birthday Central.

Your Grandma Lee was a twin, she had a set of twins (your uncles Joe and Arthur), so there was a possibility that I could follow suit. I only felt the kicks of one strong baby knowing full well that this one would grow up to be a soccer player. Ultra sound was not the norm at that time, so we had two names chosen. If a boy, Travis Adam, if a girl—Alicia Marie. No twin names were planned.

Your Grandma Schatz came to Las Vegas from Phoenix awaiting your birth. She left after two weeks, because you hadn't made your grand debut. You were now three weeks late, and Dr. Romeo was going to induce labor the next day. I had to set my mind and body on having you that very night. The fact that you were born late should not have anything to do with some sort of self-fulfilling prophecy of being late everywhere you go. Son, we need to work on that problem through hypnosis, and find out why you can't be anywhere on time.

On the night I went to the hospital, I waited for your Dad's return from the Lariat Club. The county western star, Little Jimmy Dickens, was playing there, so I encouraged Red to go.

"Are you sure you'll be okay?" he said.

"Of course, I will. Go, have a good time and enjoy yourself." When he returned shortly after midnight, I had my suitcase packed.

"Why aren't you in bed?" he scolded.

"I have someplace to go," I said with a smile.

"Where?" he blurted.

"To the hospital, honey"

"But the doctor is going to induce labor tomorrow," he said with a puzzled look.

"Yes, I know. That's why I'm going to the hospital, now. I don't want him to induce labor. It may be harmful to the baby." "Let's get your suitcase packed," he said excitedly.

"It's ready," I announced.

He helped me into the car, and wanted to run every stop light and stop sign enroute to the hospital.

"No honey, take your time, the sooner we get there, the longer the wait."

"But this is the only chance I have of running red lights," he said. "I have a good excuse. You're ready to have a baby! No police officer would write me a ticket for that."

We arrived safely without breaking the law much to your Dad's dismay. He wanted to go in the delivery room, but it was nothing that we had discussed earlier, and the answer would have been the same. "No!" I didn't want anyone to see me in pain. You were born five hours later at 6:53 a.m., twenty inches long, eight pounds six ounces, with a big foot print on the birth certificate that exceeded the space allotted. You were a darling baby, filled out nicely, no wrinkles, and beautiful red hair. As late as you were, I was surprised that you didn't have teeth. You were such a good infant—never fussy. After the first week you slept all night.

Chapter 3

When you were four months old, we flew to Wichita for Christmas to meet some of Red's brothers, sisters, and his Mom. Red flew his Cessna. When we were crossing the Rocky Mountains, I leaned over the front seat to change your diaper. Gregg was fiddling with the small window and unlatched it. The hinges were on the top so it flew up and stayed opened in that position. My butt was nearly sucked out of the window. A freezing gust of wind hit your bare bottom, and you started screaming at the top of your lungs. I had a hard time trying to get my butt back inside not to mention how it almost ripped off my skirt. Red yelled, "Close the window, quick!"

I finally pulled my butt inside then turned around in the seat and put my arm out to close it. Each time the force of the wind would flop my arm backwards like a rag doll. I thought I might lose it.

"I can't close it!" I said.

"You have to!" he insisted.

I couldn't pull my arm inside let alone reach up for the window. Finally on my third attempt, I pulled it shut. Thank you, Lord! Meanwhile, you were laying in the backseat without a diaper, freezing your buns off, and frantically screaming.

One of Red's sisters met us at the airport and we drove to Iona's house. Most of Red's family was there. They were curious to meet me. His Mother pulled him to the side and said, "Son are you feeding her? She's so thin! I don't think she could do a day's work." All of Red's family worked in the fields picking cotton. They were strong and corn fed. I guess I looked like a wimp next to them.

Red had once told me they had a few horses on the farm. The way to judge a good horse is to look at its teeth. I was a bit leery whenever one of his family members got close to me. I had made up my mind that the first person to lift my lip to check out my teeth would see me leaving the house. Although I have good teeth, a nice trait I inherited from my Mom, who still had all of her own teeth at age 93.

Chapter 4

I took birth control pills for a year which made me sick to my stomach, and gave me terrible headaches. Your Dad decided it would be easier for him to have a vasectomy than to see me sick.

I also had pernicious anemia, so Red gave me B12 and iron shots each morning for a year. Meanwhile, I came down with rheumatoid arthritis. I could barely get out of bed. I'd scoot out on my knees to the floor, then pull myself up by the cupboard door. My hands were so swollen that I couldn't put pins in your diaper, so I would struggle to put rubber pants over the diaper in the hope that the diaper would stay in place.

Dr. Rosen said, "Get used to it because you will be in a wheelchair soon." I couldn't accept that. I had always been so active.

Mom was worried about my condition. She called one evening and asked me to pick up my birthday gift at the airport. She repeated, Friday, flight #639 from Santa Monica, California. She continued, "I've paid for a rolfer to come to Las Vegas, and work on you Friday, Saturday and Sunday. Give her the guest room and feed her. Take her back to the airport Sunday evening." "Wait a minute Mom, "what's a rolfer?" I asked. "The rolfer will explain everything," said Mom.

Mom always gave unusual gifts, but this topped them all. The rolfer, named Stacey, arrived. She was a tall German woman, who worked on muscles like a chiropractor works on realigning the bones. She would find areas of the body where fascia was bunched. She would smooth it out with her elbow, and lots of pressure. After that weekend I felt like a new person. Red flew me to Santa Monica for seven more treatments before I was completely cured. She certainly had the touch of God, a real miracle worker. Since Stacey was so helpful, I asked her to look at your left foot which toed in a bit. She worked on you for twenty minutes, and your foot was perfectly straight and never toed in again. We had paid more for a pair of corrective shoes than for one treatment from Stacey.

Red wasn't sure how this rolfing worked. He was a skeptic, but she made a believer out of him. He had driven trucks for years and had constant pain between his shoulder blades. She put her elbow in his back and pressed hard, moving the elbow toward the neck. Of course, there were other things she did, but after fifteen minutes he never had another pain there.

We had asked her to work on your brothers arms, but the five breaks in his upper arms had stunted the growth. But still without her help, his arms would have been a lot worse. Somehow she stimulated a little more growth. Every time, I think about Gregg's broken arms, and being beaten by the baby sitter's husband, a minister no less, I feel sick to my stomach. Gregg was only eight months old. How could anyone do such a terrible thing?

Stacey had helped our entire family. As for me, well, I was so happy not to be crippled, or in a wheelchair as Dr. Rosen had predicted. I went back to the Dunes, dancing in the Casino de Paris show. I was a new woman.

Chapter 5

When Red and I celebrated our second anniversary, it felt like our fiftieth. You had been born, Gregg had a hernia operation, Red was audited by the IRS, and had to make monthly payments for a year. I had bouts of rheumatoid arthritis and anemia. Red was laid off at the test site, and had to go to Grand Junction, Colorado to find work. Thank goodness, when he called an old boss, where he had previously been employed, he was told he could come back to the Arapahoe Drilling Company to work. The pay was not much, but something was better than nothing.

I felt like a military wife, holding down the fort until Red returned.

Due to past experiences, he had a real problem trusting women. He also saw several of his good friends go through ugly divorces, where the wives took the husbands for everything they had. He kept the checking account in his name and paid all the bills when they were due. That presented a problem when he left the state to work. He would send me a money order, but, then I would have to cash it, and go to each utility company, and pay the bill in cash. Finally, after being married to Red over two years, he said, "Sweet, I think you better get your name on the checking account now."

Travis, it took your Dad that long to have trust in me. Actually, it hurt my feelings since I had never given him any reason not to trust me.

When you were two years old, we would say to you, "Silly Clown," and you would roll your eyes up in your head, stick your tongue to the side of your mouth, and make a funny face. You were so comical. You started doing that at the grocery store unbeknownst to me, without any prompting. People would look at me with sympathy thinking you were mentally challenged until one day I caught you making weird faces and rolling your eyes up. I then understood why I got such sympathetic looks from the other shoppers. But all I had to say to you was, "Travis, that's not nice to fool other people in thinking you aren't right in the head.

Please don't do that at the store." You stopped making faces after that. You were really such a good child. I rarely had to scold you.

When you were still two years old and Gregg was five, I was awakened one morning by shills of laughter. What on earth was going on? I asked myself, as I hurried out of bed. I quietly crept down the hallway and peered around the door frame into the kitchen. There was some sort of slime on your feet, toes, legs, and arms. You and your brother were only wearing underwear. When you spotted me, you momentarily got quiet, then burst into another uncontrollable laugh.

"Oh Mom," you said, "We are having a great time. Watch us." One by one you ran onto the slippery tile floor and slid on your bottoms as if on a water slide, and you didn't stop, until your feet hit the refrigerator at the far end of the kitchen. "That's just great," I said, sarcastically. "Please tell me, what on earth is that stuff oozing between your toes, all over your body, and on the floor?"

"Mom, they are the old bananas that were sitting on the kitchen counter. You didn't want to save them, did you?" said Gregg.

"Yes, I was going to make banana nut bread."

"But Mom," Gregg said, "Travis tried to peel one and it fell on the floor. He tried to pick it up several times but stepped in it. He got another one, but it fell apart too. He kept looking for a good one to eat, but they were all bad and kept falling out of his hand. He was slipping in the mess, so we just decided to mash them between our toes. Hey Mom, we made up a new game."

"Yeah, I can see, so what did you call it? Monkey see Monkey do?" Maybe this was how wine came into being—some kids started smashing grapes between their toes for fun, I thought.

"Sorry boys your fun is over, now you have to clean the floor."

I got a bucket of soapy water and two small towels "Get busy cleaning." Actually, I didn't know what should come first, cleaning the slime off of you, or cleaning the floor. If I cleaned you first then you would get goopy again while washing the floor. Then, if you mopped the floor first you would continue to track the bananas all over the place from your feet. I looked at the clock and yelled, "Oh my heavens, it is seven o'clock and I have to be at the airport to pick up your aunts flying in from Wichita. Then I heard my alarm clock sounding. I ran to the bedroom, turned it off, and returned to the kitchen. Now my dilemma was partially solved. You and Gregg had poured the entire bucket of water on the kitchen floor, and resumed your fun by slipping and sliding in the soapy water.

"Look Mom," you said, full of excitement, we are taking a bath the same time we are cleaning the floor. The next hour was like fast forwarding a movie.

When your Dad came in from work, after his graveyard shift, he said. "Hi boys, Are you ready to go to the airport? I see you are all dressed up and looking sharp" He looked over at me and said, "Honey, why aren't you ready?"

"It's a long story, give me a minute, and I'll tell you about it on the way to the airport." In the car we had a radio station playing Oldies but Goodies and a Chuck Berry song came on, "Too Much Monkey Business," Then after that came Little Richard's "Slipping and a Sliding" (Peeping and a Hiding) that hit the nail on the head, as I relayed the boy's morning antics to Red.

Travis, as you got older, you worried too much. We would leave for the grocery store, but before arriving you would say, "Mom, did you lock the door? Mom, did you turn off the coffee pot? Mom do you have enough money for the groceries?"

"Yes Travis, please don't worry about it." But it was useless, you worried anyway.

You were crushed when Gregg started school. Each morning you stood outside and watched him walk off. You wanted to go with him. The following year as you watched him go with his friends from the neighborhood, you came up with a business idea. You made toast with butter and jelly and sold it for a nickel to the kids walking past the house on their way to school. You were only four.

As you grew older you not only had good ideas, but you were electrically minded as well as mechanically inclined. We would give you a broken blender, or electric can opener, and somehow you figured out how to make it work again. You even changed the cord on the iron for me.

Every time you got into your Dad's pick-up truck, you pretended you were riding a motorcycle. You would twist your wrists and verbally reeve up the imaginary engine. On one of our family vacations to Wichita, you reeved the engine of a motorcycle the entire trip, twelve hundred miles. Travis, you were not only tired, but your voice was very hoarse.

We kept the radio playing trying to drown out the noise.

Chapter 6

Red and I finally had a honeymoon five years after we were married. My stepfather, Bud, died the day we were married, so that was no time for a celebration. Mom called to tell us that they would not be driving over from Phoenix for our wedding. Bud had a freak accident. He had cataract surgery and being disoriented; he fell out of bed, had a stroke and died. That was shocking news.

We had very little money when we married, but after saving for five years, we could afford a honeymoon. We flew to Mazatlan in our plane and spent a glorious week. You and Gregg spent the week in Phoenix with your grandma.

With Red having an airplane, it allowed us to go many places. We flew to Michigan to see Grandpa Boop, to Ohio to see my Dad, to Wichita and Omaha to see Red's family and Phoenix to see Mom.

I had decided to go to work when you started kindergarten. Red was working too many hours trying to make ends meet, and it wasn't fair. I needed to pitch in and help financially. I saw an ad in the newspaper that the phone company was hiring operators. I called to inquire about an application and appointment to take a test. On the day I was scheduled to go, I dropped you off at Trinity Church, daycare. I explained to you that I would be back soon. You cried and screamed, "Don't go Mommy! Don't leave me!" You held onto the gate trying to open it to run after me. One of the nursery teachers said, "Go on, he'll be okay in a few minutes." But I could still hear you screaming as I got in the car.

"Mommy, don't go. Please don't leave me. I'll be a good boy."

I drove off with tears in my eyes feeling like a terrible Mom. I wondered if it was worth going to work, if I had to face this emotional separation each day. The test took longer than anticipated. As I pulled into the church parking lot my heart sunk. You were still by the gate exhausted from crying, only a faint whimper was left. Your little eyes were so red. The nursery school teacher said that she was not able to distract you from the gate. You never left that spot for three hours. You waited and watched while other parents came to pick up their children, and I was the last to pick you up.

"You were never coming back to get me" you said, pathetically, in between sobs.

"Sure I was, Travis. Don't be angry. I had to look for a job. I was coming back for you."

"No," you cried, "I waited and waited, but you didn't show up."

"But sweetheart, I'm here now." I hugged you and told you that I loved you, but no reassurance helped. You just kept repeating, pitifully, "I thought that you were never coming back to get me. All the other parents came to get their kids but not you. Mommy, I waited but you were the last one. Why did you leave me so long?"

Travis, you were extremely distraught and upset. I was never able to apologize enough. Saying, "I'm sorry," just didn't get it. I wondered how a parent could give up a child for adoption, without such traumatic consequences on both sides. I wondered how a military parent would go off to war, and possibly never return. What a terrible feeling of abandonment for the child. It would stay with him the rest of his life.

Travis, anytime we had a disagreement you would bring up the incident. "You left me at the church and wasn't coming back to get me." You brought this up throughout grade school, high school, and even your early adult years. It was a dark indelible mark on your heart that you would not forget. You may not have forgiven me yet, but I think you understand now that you are a father.

Chapter 7

One year my birthday fell on Easter. As a surprise, Red took both you and your brother to the bakery. He ordered a special cake with a bunny rabbit in fluffy white coconut flakes, and multi—colored jelly beans arranged in the grass, which was spikes of green icing. When Red brought the cake home he set it on the dining room table. You and Gregg were tempted by the jelly beans and ate one or two every time you passed the table. When I arrived home from work, I noticed the cake right away. You heard me coming in the front door, so you ran in the dining room, and yelled, "SUPRISE!" But the surprise was on Red. He looked bewildered. I laughed hysterically. You and your brother had eaten all the colored jelly beans except the black licorice ones, which were piled up by the rabbit's tail. Red blurted, "Honestly, honey, I didn't buy the cake that way. When I brought it home it had all colors of jelly beans as Easter eggs," he explained.

"I'm sure you didn't buy it like that," I said smiling, but you must admit, it is unique. We all had a good laugh.

It never failed that the day before school pictures were to be taken, you and Gregg would think of something mischievous to do to each other. One year you tried to cut his hair while he was sleeping, cutting out chunks by the hairline. In retaliation, he took numerous colored marking pens and painted your face all different shades while you slept. Nothing would take it off. I tried cold cream, baby oil, Vaseline, even fingernail polish remover, but to no avail.

Remember when your Dad was a pilot for Apache Airlines? Since he worked in Phoenix, we would only see him on the weekends when he flew home. We would drive to the airport and park by the perimeter fence in the dark. While we waited for him, you and Gregg always wanted me to tell you a spooky story. My mother always told my sisters and I stories which helped spark our imagination. The scarier the story, the better you liked it. As we watched the planes land we waited for a white and aqua blue Dehavelin Dove or a four engine Heron. When it landed, and the passengers departed, we would then welcome your Dad home.

There never seemed to be enough time spent with your Dad. I was happy when the Boy Scouts planned a father-son Cake Bake. It was the bi-centennial year. Nevada was 200 years old. You and your Dad designed three cakes. They were side by side. The first one was shaped like the number two, and it had red icing, the second one was round like a zero and it had white icing, the third was also shaped like a zero and it had blue icing. The cakes portrayed two hundred years. In the background of the cake tray was a picture of the American flag. The cakes were raffled off at the end of the meeting to raise money for the scouts. The other kids had one cake, but you had three for the price of one. It was a nice afternoon that you and Red spent baking. Every chance of being together was important.

Chapter 8

I registered you and your brother at Cragin pool for swimming classes during the summer. I wanted you both to take each class twice to make sure you got the basics. You did and both of you are good swimmers today. I remember how you and Gregg bulked, "Mom, we have the first class in the morning, and the water is so cold." But you toughed it out and I was happy about that.

I was so pleased one day when you came home from the lake, and thanked me for giving you swimming lessons, because you realized how important it was to know how to swim, especially having a boat, and being around water. I think one of your friends almost drowned that day in the lake. I thought extracurricular activities were important, so you got a variety: Cartoon drawing, karate, drum lessons, motocross bike racing, soccer, and skateboarding. Travis, you really excelled in all you did.

You loved motocross bike racing, and you were good at it. You planned on getting in a certain lane before the race began, and you calculated the speed and abilities of the other contestants. You won many trophies.

You were also a wonderful soccer player. Fast and agile. You played for the Condors and the Spurs. Again, you won trophies. I loved going to your games to cheer you on. It reminded me of my high school years when I was a cheerleader.

We had a dog named Boots. He was a good-natured Labrador retriever with just one drawback. Whenever he saw you and Gregg playing in the living room, he wanted to join in the fun. He would take a flying leap through the window ending up inside, uninjured, wagging his tail. After Red replaced the glass three times, he said, "That's it, the dog goes to the pound."

Gregg piped up and said, "If the dog goes to the pound, I go too." You spoke up and said, "If my brother and the dog go to the pound, I go too. Needless to say, we kept Boots. We couldn't lose our family. After returning from vacation, one year, the gate had been left open by the fellow feeding him, and Boots had run away. We checked at the pound, but he wasn't there. I'm sure you thought that it had been prearranged, but it wasn't.

Most of the time you and your brother stuck together, but that's not saying that there weren't occasions when you pushed his buttons. Each time we sat down at the table to eat dinner, Gregg would yell, "Stop it Trav!" I'd look at you and you were just eating as if nothing happened. Gregg would yell again then say, "Mom, he's showing me the food in his mouth, and it's disgusting. Make him stop!" I'd look over at you and you innocently shrugged your shoulders like you didn't have the foggiest notion of what Gregg was talking about. Finally, I caught you doing it, and told you to stop or leave the table. Each night you proceeded to aggravate your brother in the same manner. You finally outgrew that stage. Thank goodness.

Then Gregg would be the instigator. He loved to give you "murphy's," by pulling your jeans up to the middle of your chest. He also tickled you until you peed your pants. That certainly embarrassed you, especially in front of your friends.

You and your brother were as different as night and day. Gregg always had an interest in hunting. You did not. You didn't even like the "good luck, rabbit's foot." You would say. "Well, that wasn't very lucky for the rabbit, who lost his foot for a stupid key chain!"

When you boys wanted to go swimming, I would say, "You can go after your rooms are cleaned." Gregg would run in his room and start hanging up his clothes.

Travis, you would call out to me in five minutes, "I'm all finished Mom, you can come in an inspect it." Gregg would barely start on tidying up his room. He would be mad at you for being done so fast. I didn't find out until you were grown-up that you shoved everything under your bed, and I didn't check there.

Chapter 9

You took over your brother's paper route even though you weren't old enough. The circulation boss thought you could do it and you did. You would porch the papers of the invalids. You were conscientious and reliable. You hated collecting at the end of the month, because no one wanted to pay. They used all kinds of excuses for not paying what was owed. Their bill would come out of your wages. It was lifting the heavy Sunday papers onto your bike handlebars that aggravated and caused your hernia. You had surgery to repair it.

One day while your Aunt Pat and Uncle Joe were visiting, you came storming into the house, before your paper route was finished. You were yelling all sorts of obscenities in front of your relatives. "The f … Mexican around the corner just sucker punched me for kicking his dog away from my bike. He knocked me down. His dog always runs after me and tries to bite my leg, and the owner won't do anything about it." You were so angry at your Dad for not going over to settle the score. I'm not sure a fight would have resolved anything, except some satisfaction that your Dad stood up for you. Red probably would have ended up in jail. Your Dad was so embarrassed that you used such foul language in front of his brother and sister-in law that he wouldn't listen to a thing you said, until you apologized to them. That just wasn't going to happen. You were too mad. But it wasn't your fault that the dog tried to bite you, or the ignorant man hit you. I was furious, too. I wanted to tear that jerk apart for picking on an eleven-year-old just doing his job. Red told me to stay out of it. He realized that I would probably get hit or go to jail. You phoned the police. They needed to know the exact address and the man's name which I was determined to get for you. Nothing ever happened to the complaint, and you never had your day of reckoning—Not with the neighbor or your Dad. You and your Dad weren't as close after that incident. Maybe by now, you have forgiven him. The neighbor was ignorant when it came to making up his dog mind. He rarely kept the dog inside the gate per the city ordinance.

Red brought home a German shepherd from one of our rental apartments. The new tenant knew we didn't allow dogs, so when he got caught, he gave his dog to Red. You and Gregg named the dog Chief. Red liked the dog but there was a problem. The dog had a hernia. I said, "We are not dealing with anymore hernias." Gregg had an inguinal hernia, and you had an umbilical hernia. I was not going to pay for another operation, especially for a dog just given to us. The dog had to go to the pound and right away before you formed any attachments to him.

You often said, "Mom, when I grow up, I'm going to buy you a sewing machine."

"Why, Son? I don't sew."

"Every mother needs a sewing machine," you said.

"Thank you for the nice thought, but I don't need one." For years you were adamant about getting a sewing machine for me. I couldn't figure that out. I guess if I had a daughter, I would need a sewing machine to make dresses but having boys, all I did was patch. You finally bought one for yourself when you spotted a good buy at a yard sale. You started sewing and even made pillowcases for me. You later got an industrial machine to make headliners and upholstery for your VW.

You were always kind to birds and animals. You would try to mend a bird's foot after it fell out of its nest. Once you ran after a mouse that only had his tail caught in the mouse trap. You yelled at it. "Come back here, you can't run off with the mouse trap!" You chased it from the garage to Banjo Circle with a broom. I was laughing so hard at you. Finally, you got it stopped but you couldn't kill it. You released its tail and let the mouse run toward the desert.

Chapter 10

I think a low time in your youth was when you had to wear braces on your teeth and kids called you "metal mouth." That was rude. Besides, it hurt whenever you had to have them tightened.

You didn't like being thin either, but it was healthier than being fat. Your pet peeve was all the advertising done for overweight people, and no ads or products for the underweight. I recalled when you asked a girl on a date, and she told you to ask her later, after you gained twenty pounds. How cruel is that! I told you never to ask that girl out again.

It didn't help when your Dad, jokingly, said to me, "Don't buy Trav striped pajamas, because he'll only end up with one stripe."

Your self-esteem was waning. I was glad when you picked up a few good traits from your Dad. You learned at a young age how to barter, which made you more confident. You would play a game of pool with your friend Eric for motor oil for your cycle. To this very day, you have survived through bartering.

One afternoon, your Dad and his friend, Bill, were talking in the garage. All of a sudden you bolted into the kitchen announcing, "Dad knows how to cuss! I just heard him use bad words."

I laughed and replied, "Son, your Dad has always known how to cuss, but he simply has too much respect for women and children to cuss in their presence. I hope you keep that in mind as you get older." For the most part, that good trait stuck with you and Gregg.

One Saturday, I was attending a luncheon at a friend's house. When the doorbell rang, the hostess answered only to find a police officer inquiring if Mrs. Lee was there. Mrs. Jacobs came into the dining room and said, "It's for you," Then grimaced. "It's the police, she whispered." As I hurried to the door, Officer Longo met me with a smile and a wink." I have your son in the back seat of the patrol car. Dispatch received a call from a security officer at the Chevrolet dealership stating that someone was shooting at him from the desert area. I found the boys shooting off firecrackers. Rather than take them to juvenile detention, I told them I would take them to their parents. I just dropped the other boy at his house. Your son told me that you weren't home, but a few blocks away, so I'll leave him with you and let you handle it from here.

"Thank you, officer. Thanks a million."

I thought of some of the antics I pulled as a kid and was lucky not to have a police record. One night, my friends and I threw cow manure at cars, never realizing the ramifications if one wrecked. We hit the windshield of a police car not seeing the lights on top, until it was too late. When the spotlight hit us, we tried to run, but got caught and went to jail. We were fifteen years old, and full of mischief to put it mildly. We smelled so bad that the drunks stayed up against one wall begging the sheriff to move us out of the cell. I had on a hooded sweatshirt, and whenever I leaned over, more crap fell out of the hood onto the cell floor. My friend, Karen, had been behind me, during our caper, and never knew when I was going to raise back up with another handful of manure from the bag. I took a few mushy hits to the side of the head. It filled up my hoodie. Mom came to bail us out and was furious. Not that we pulled a prank like that, but that we were dumb enough to get caught.

I worried when I put my application in for the police department in Las Vegas. Would they uncover my teenage pranks, when doing a background check on me? Evidently, there was nothing on the books— No rap sheet so to speak. Luckily, I came from a small town with little crime, and where everyone knew each other.

Chapter 11

There was a new family that moved into the neighborhood from Kentucky. One of the girls was about your age. She was a heavy-set girl with a complex, because she usually walked with her head down. She always looked sad. If I was in the front yard, I'd say, "hello" To her. She would look up momentarily and nod. I asked you what her name was, and you told me "Orca." The next day when I saw her coming home from school, I waved and said, "Hello Orca." She ran home crying. Oh, good heavens, what did I do to upset her?

When you arrived home, I told you what happened.

"Oh, no Mom, please tell me that you didn't call her Orca."

"I did, Travis. Isn't that what you told me her name was?"

"Mom, Orca is a whale! I thought you knew that."

"No, I didn't. Good grief! I really hurt her feelings. I'll have to apologize to her.

What an awkward situation this is!"

I was at work when I received a strange phone call from you. There was panic in your voice. "Mom, someone stole the carport!"

"What do you mean?" I said in disbelief. "How could that happen?"

"I don't know Mom, it was there when I left for school but it's not here now."

"Come on son, you are pulling my leg"

"No Mom, I'm serious. The entire carport is gone."

I thought Travis loves playing jokes on people, but this seemed to be real.

"Son is the wind blowing hard?"

"Not a bit Mom, it's calm."

"Okay, Travis, start at the beginning, and tell me exactly what happened.

"Well, Mike and I were walking home from school, talking about our new teacher. I was a block from the house, when I looked down at the street at our driveway. It was bare. There was no carport. Mike said that it could have been repossessed like his dad's car, if we were behind on the payments. Are we behind, Mom?"

"No," I said. "We paid in full when it was installed. We don't owe any money." We were not living in an affluent neighborhood, most of the residents were blue collar workers, like us. I could understand where Mike was coming from.

"Son, do all the other houses on the block look okay? Are there any tree limbs in the street?"

"No, Mom, there is no debris."

Wait a minute Travis, let's be realistic. It took two days to erect the carport, therefore it would take hours to dismantle it." This was not a free-standing carport. It was eighteen by twenty-four feet and attached on two sides of the house. There would be hundreds of the nuts and bolts to remove, plus the support beams and the aluminum sections of the roof. Certainly, one of our neighbors would have questioned any suspicious action like that, if someone was trying to steal it.

"Trav, if my boss will let me off early, I'm coming home. Meanwhile don't worry about it. Do your homework. I'll see you soon. We'll solve this mystery."

As I pulled in the driveway, I saw several vehicles from Nevada Power Company at the end of the street. I stepped out of my car and noticed that the bolts from the carport were still in the concrete but completely stripped, and two large flower pots were missing. I stuck my head in the front door and said, "I'm home, Trav. I'm going to walk around the block and find out if anyone saw what happened."

"Wait Mom, I'll go with you," you said, as you came running toward the door. We walked to the corner then around the cul-de-sac. I saw a young couple who recently moved to the neighborhood. Their hands outstretched and open as if to say, "What happened?" My thoughts, exactly.

"Lose something?" said Mr. Chambers.

"Yes," I said nervously.

"Well, it's been found in this young couple's back yard. Part of it tore a hole in their roof, and the rest is hanging over the kids swing set where the children were playing." When I walked to their back yard and saw the sharp pieces of aluminum teetering from the top bar of the swing, I realized that is was a miracle it didn't crash down on the children, and cut them in half. They could have also been electrocuted by downed power lines hanging over the swing. I looked up and said a quick prayer. "Thank you, Lord, for sparing these two little girls."

Another neighbor walked over and said, "While I was watering my grass, a ferocious dust devil kicked up just out of nowhere. It only hit your driveway, sucking up your carport which went flying like a magic carpet over the roof tops, then disappeared around the corner. I ran out in the street and saw sparks like the Fourth of July and realized that the arcing was due to the downed power lines. I called Nevada Power right away."

I thought to myself, the carport can be replaced, and the neighbor's roof repaired but had those two precious little girls been injured or killed, it would have been such a tragedy. I said another prayer that evening, because I was so grateful it wasn't worse.

Chapter 12

One night your Dad's partner called in sick, so he was assigned to a different area to work. He couldn't work the Westside, without being in a two-man police unit. Red was assigned to our neighborhood. That is never a good plan. If you have to arrest your neighbor, there can be severe repercussions and vindictiveness. Your Dad had to arrest a bad kid on a burglary charge, who lived three blocks from us. He knew Red and our family. In retribution, he threatened, "I'll beat up your boys, rape your wife, and burn down your house." Red asked you and your brother to walk home from school with other kids to be safe. The thief made good on one of his promises. He tried to burn down our house. We found numerous pieces of charred newspaper in a stack of firewood we kept piled along the side of our home. He had failed in his endeavor. Thank goodness. We could never prove that it was him, nevertheless he spent a lot of time in jail on various burglary and vandalism charges.

One evening you said, "Dad, can I borrow your pickup truck tonight?" Red had plans, but said, "Go ahead, son, I'll get a ride with my friend. Unbeknownst to you, Red was going to the strip to walk a picket line. Your Dad, as a strong union member, was involved with helping the culinary union strike at the MGM. That evening you and your high school friends decided to cruise the strip. When you saw a big crowd of people in front of the MGM picketing, supposedly, your friends decided to spray them with a large fire extinguisher filled with water that you had in the truck. After they were blasted with water, you drove off. What were you thinking? Someone took down the license plate and called Metro. The following day, when Red returned to work, he was called into the captain's office requesting an explanation, "Why did you spray the picketers in front of the MGM last night?" Red answered in a state of shock. "I don't know what you're talking about." The captain continued, "Dispatch got a call last night at 6:45 p.m., someone with a fire extinguisher was spraying the picketers. The license plate that was reported came back to your vehicle, and you as the registered owner. What do you have to say for yourself?"

"I was at the MGM last night walking the picket line, but I didn't start until

7:00 p.m. When I came on my assigned shift, I heard some disgruntled union members speaking about someone spraying them a few minutes earlier. They figured it was management trying to discourage them from picketing. Captain, I can assure you that it wasn't me. Why would I spray the people I was trying to support? I can give you a whole list of people that can verify what I was doing last night. Whoever called in the license plate must have been off a number or two."

"Okay," said the captain," you're dismissed."

When Red got home, he questioned you about the prior evening. He knew you had a fire extinguisher, and also had his truck. "Son, that made me look bad in light of trying to help out the strikers. In addition, I was called on the carpet at work about that incident. I couldn't believe you would do such a thing."

You convinced your Dad that you couldn't possibly drive and hold a big fire extinguisher at the same time. "Dad, it was my two friends in the back of the truck who pulled that trick. I'm innocent, really I am! I didn't know they were going to spray the picketers."

Your Dad's reaction was just as you expected. "You were up to no good when you left the house with the fire extinguisher," said Red. "You wouldn't have taken it if you didn't have an ulterior motive."

13

On March 4th, 1980, just after midnight, two officers came to the house with bad news. Your Dad, as a police officer, had been shot in the head. I left you and Gregg a note in case you woke up, before I returned home.

"Boys, I'm at the hospital. Your Dad has been hurt. I'll come back for you after I find out how he's doing." Love, Mom

I kept thinking, Red was only forty-two years old. There was so much more for us to do together. I prayed, "Please Lord, don't let him die."

You were a freshman and Gregg was a senior in high school. You and your brother need your Dad, especially now, during your teenage years for guidance, advice, and to pass on his good work ethic.

A few hours later an officer drove me home to get my car, and wake you with the disturbing news. You and your brother didn't go to school for a few days instead you stayed at the hospital with me. I don't know what was going through your mind but your questions were probably the same as mine.

"Will he live? Will he have brain damage? Will he be able to recognize anyone?" These were my concerns, too.

When the bullet pierced through his jaw, he evidently, bit down slowing the momentum. It sheared off half of his teeth and broke his jaw in eight places. It destroyed his saliva gland on the left side. His squad gave him a food processor to pulverize his meals. He could forcibly push a straw inside his mouth and suck up his nutrition. Recovery took a long time. He couldn't open his mouth for a year. Meanwhile his teeth abscessed. They were poisoning him. The dentist had to break his jaw again to do the necessary dental work. He went back to work in three months with a bullet still lodged in the back of his head just above the spinal column, so close that it could have paralyzed him. He had ruptured discs in his lower back, where he was kicked after being shot. He had a total of five surgeries, all the aftermath of the shooting. For three years, he spent most of his time at doctor appointments, physical therapists, and the dentist.

I, too, was a cop at the time, but couldn't jeopardize being shot on the job. I had been fighting city hall, but it was a losing battle.

I transferred to the airport where I could keep a low profile. I didn't know what residual effects Red would have, so I had to be able to earn double the money. I kicked in the after burner by going back to college to get my degree in psychology. I opened my own business called "Motivation Unlimited," and worked two jobs for seven years.

July 2, 1987, at age fifty, Red had a heart attack. Your Dad has been through so much, but you will never hear him complaining about his health. He just keeps on trucking!

He, with a great attitude, lived by the bible verse in Proverbs (17:22), "A cheerful heart is a good medicine, but a downcast spirit dries up the bones."

I think that you and Gregg resented the fact your Dad and I worked so hard. You called us workaholics, but our rationale was to earn as much as we could, while we were still able. That would allow us to have a comfortable retirement. We should have spent more time with you and your brother, but as teenagers you were busy with your friends.

Chapter 14

On weekends Red and I usually went to yard sales. One Saturday upon returning home, there was a message on our phone recorder.

"Mrs. Lee, this is Tim. I took Travis to the hospital with a broken wrist. He fell while we were skateboarding. You need to come to the hospital to sign for treatment."

We panicked, as we called the University Medical Center's emergency room, but you weren't there. We called Sunrise Hospital then North Las Vegas Hospital and Rose de Lima. You weren't at any of them. Where were you, we wondered. Then, I remembered that Tim had once worked at Valley Hospital, so I called there. Bingo. By the time we arrived, your arm had swollen so badly that the doctor was unable to set it. I thought if only we had cell phones back in those days, we would be able to quickly contact someone, and vice versa, in the case of an emergency. Our response time would be fast. Cell phones were a great invention. The next day you saw an orthopedic surgeon, who put five pins in your wrist. They looked like the pins you put in a turkey before lacing it up. The flexibility of your wrist and your drumming career was on the line. After your wrist healed, it was difficult to bend it to play the guitar and the drums. This was your dominant hand that you broke. Fortunately, you are ambidextrous, which is a good trait. You use both sides of your brain making you smarter than the average bear, although your doctor didn't think so. He got angry with you for spray painting your cast, purple. "That was a dumb thing to do," he said. There were many autographs and pictures drawn on it. The doctor worried about infection from the paint but the paint hadn't penetrated through the plaster of Paris cast.

After your wrist healed, you found a project to work on. You spotted a small homemade boat that was for sale, at a neighborhood yard sale. Since you liked boats, you bought it. It only cost eight dollars. You sanded it down, fiber glassed it in the garage, then added a coat of paint. It was a long drawn-out process and fiber glassing was so stinky.

Your Dad and I kept saying, "NOAH, when are the rains coming? Is your boat finished yet?" We teased you a lot about your skiff, then one day it was complete, and you wanted to find out if it was sea worthy. Before taking it to the lake, you put it in the neighbor's swimming pool but it wouldn't stay afloat. It sank. You were disappointed after spending so much time on it. I was glad the rains didn't come.

You loved vehicles just like your Dad. He liked big vehicles and you liked fast ones. You rode quads and go carts. Now you were old enough to buy a car. You bought your first car from one of your soccer coaches. It was a tan Baja bug. You later bought another VW and had it painted aqua blue. It was a beauty. After selling that one, you got another one and painted it yellow. Your cars were spiffy. You knew a lot about fixing them up. We were pleased that you kept busy with mechanical repairs and constructive projects.

You got a job working at K-Mart. You learned how to operate the forklift when you worked in the garden department, then you learned to use the cash registers. You looked so nice when you went to work, with your white shirt, slacks and a necktie. Since you had a paycheck coming in, you and your Dad went shopping for a nice boat. You bought a new red and white Sea Ray. Little did you know that the payments would go on for twelve years. It should have only been six years, but you didn't have much money for a down payment. Your monthly obligation needed to be affordable and within your means. It meant that with the interest you paid over the years, you could have had a yacht. The whole idea of making payments on something nice was you would be able to enjoy the lake, and have something to show for your money rather than throw it away on drugs, or any other bad habit that kids your age might get into. There were lots of expenses related to the boat so you didn't enjoy it as much as we hoped. That was your first loan and payment plan to establish credit which didn't turn out like we had planned. Your Dad was the co— signer, and the boat ended up on his credit report and not yours. He had plenty of credit, you needed to have some. At least you enjoyed the boat for about five or six years, and took it to Lake Mead often.

Chapter 15

You asked your Dad if he would like to drive the motorhome to Parker, Arizona to watch the boat and ski races that your friends were in. Your friend, Mike, offered to take Red and I on a ride before the race began but we thought not.

"Go, Mom and Dad," you pleaded. "You may never have another chance to go on such a fast cigarette boat." We stepped on board, the engine revved, then we were off like a bat out of hell. We went so fast that I couldn't see the shoreline. It was all a blur. I tried to talk, but my face was drawn back and frozen in a half paralytic smile. The boat slapped hard against the water and the wakes. We returned to the dock, and were grateful to once again be on solid ground. I felt like I had run a jack hammer all day. I was shaky and unsteady for a while.

Fifteen minutes before the race. Mike came running over to the motorhome yelling "Travis, Travis, you have to help us. Kevin hasn't shown up. You'll have to ski in his place. We don't want to forfeit the race or our entry fee.

"Whoa," you said, "I'm just a recreational skier, not a professional. I haven't even skied for a year, and never behind a cigarette boat going 110 miles an hour."

"You can do it," said Mike. "We really need you to do this." So feeling pressured-you agreed to the insane proposal. The race began and off you went, jumping the wakes of the other boats, while trying to keep from going head over heels into the water. I watched through the binoculars. The three mile loop of the race was almost complete but the boats didn't slow down, they started around the loop again then a third, fourth, and fifth time. Oh, good heavens, how are you able to take it so long. You were holding onto the rope for dear life. My heart went out to you. You had such a frozen grimace on your face. I passed the binocular to your Dad. I kept praying though the entire race.

"Lord, keep him safe from harm."

"When is this darn race going to end?" Red said. "How is he even standing upright?" Then finally, we heard the engines cut back and the boats headed to the dock. Thank heavens, it's over. You let go of the ski rope and lay in a dead man's prone position, floating atop the water. Red and I went over to the dock as they were announcing the results of the race. Your team came in third, but that didn't matter to us. You were so relieved that the race was finished. I imagine that you vowed to never get pressured into anything again, without knowing all the facts ahead of time and how many laps it would entail.

"Oh, Dad," you said, "my legs are noodled." No one told me it was a fifteen mile race, probably, because I would have refused to do it. I wanted to let go of the rope, but I didn't want to be run over by the speed boats along side of me.

"Son, do you think you can make it to the motorhome?"

"No, not yet, Dad. Let me just rest here in the water for a little while until I can feel my arms. They are still aching as well as my legs."

Your body jerked uncontrollably from muscle fatigue. I don't know what sort of pep talk you gave yourself each time you started around another loop. Whatever you said worked. Through pain and perseverance you endured the race. To us, you were the hero of the day, no matter where you placed in the race.

Red wanted to take you and Gregg fishing for Christmas one year. Airline tickets were purchased, and off you went to visit Stan in Tacoma, Washington. Well, the trip was a calamity. It was so cold that it snowed as you were trolling for salmon in the Puget Sound. Gregg was the only one to get a small salmon. Your Dad caught a mallard duck, Stan caught a fish hook in his hand, and you caught a cold. We figured that the one and only salmon cost us about $1800.

We wanted you and your brother to see what Red did in Carson City. He was lobbying at the time. We were so proud of both of you looking so spiffy in your new suits and ties. You looked all grown up and dignified. For you and your brother, being dressed up in a suit was a rare occasion, unfortunately. On Saturday, we took you to Lake Tahoe skiing and the next day to a fancy restaurant named "Adele's" for dinner. It was the last time I saw either of you in a suit except for your weddings. I sure miss seeing you dressed up.

Red and I hoped that you would go to college but that was not in your plans. We took the money set aside for college and spent it traveling. I hope you know that it's never too late to go to college. I didn't graduate until I was 45 years old. You can be more focused on what you want when you are older. There are several important things I learned from going to college—time management, priorities, and self-discipline. Professors give so much homework that you must decide what to do first. It might be the weekend, and you want to party, but unless your school work is done—you can't. There will be no playing around when there is a term paper due, two books to read, and an exam on Monday. It's called "deferred gratification." You give up things right now, so you can enjoy the fruits of your labor, later. It's like paying your dues forward. College, vocational schools, and special talents add to your assets. A variety of experiences add to your worth on a resume. Learn whatever you can from whomever you can. Everyone has something of value they can pass on to you. Pick their brain and ask many questions. The practical knowledge you acquire will be priceless.

Chapter 16

I thought that dating was probably awkward for you since you lived at home and had no privacy. When the house next door went up for sale, I wanted to buy it. You could live there in the short term and later it would be available for Grandpa Jim or Grandma Schatz when they could no longer take care of themselves. I didn't want you moving across town. If you lived next door, I could look out the kitchen window and see who was coming and going. I just couldn't cut the apron strings. Living next door worked out fine until one of our police friends patrolling the area said that it appeared that stolen property was being taken inside, during a surveillance. That did not set well with us and we were very upset, even though you said it was one of your roommates.

We responded angrily, "Get rid of the roommates, this can't be happening! You could go to jail!" Think about the old Pennsylvania Dutch proverb, "A man is known by the company he keeps."

We only charged a minimal amount of rent that your roommates shared. Your Dad and I hoped you would learn to budget for utilities. The rent was not always paid on time but we didn't charge a late fee. The financial arrangements didn't work out so well.

Chapter 17

We were glad when you went to work for the Clark County Road Department and worked your way up the ladder. You now had insurance, vacation leave, and best of all a retirement plan.

Your girlfriend, Connie was working as assistant manager at a bank. You and Connie had decided to get married in June but the legislature wasn't over yet. Since I was retired, I spent my time in Carson City with Red. The session would not end for several more weeks. We flew to Las Vegas from Carson City for the wedding. It had been planned so nicely by both of you and economically as well. You had it catered by a Mexican restaurant and you rented the margarita machines for the drinks.

While in Carson City, I went shopping for a pretty dress to wear and luckily I found an aqua blue dress that matched a purse and heels I already had. Better yet, it was only two dollars at the thrift store. After our flight to Las Vegas, we headed to the Tropicana Hotel. Upon arrival for the wedding, the bride's mother and maid of honor were wearing aqua blue dresses. Wow, how intuitive was that? It was as though we had gotten together ahead of time to discuss what color we would be wearing.

When Connie was expecting a baby, you were thinking of names for your son. I was so tickled when you told me what you were thinking of naming him, although it was inappropriate, unless he was going to be in show business.

Red said, "Oh, don't give him a funny name, give him a normal name. Avoid initials, because he'll have trouble all his life with it like I have had with mine. Two letters for my first name has always been confusing to others."

Trav, you heeded your Dad's advice. When the baby was born, you named him Zackary James. I love that name.

You were such a wonderful Dad. We were very proud of you. One day while visiting us, you were sucking on an ice cube in your hand. Zack was in your arms, and leaned over to lick it which you allowed him to do. The ice cube got stuck on his tongue. You panicked, and Zack started crying. The harder you tried to get it off, the louder he screamed. Finally it came off and you couldn't apologize enough. Oh, you bounced him and kissed him over and over saying how sorry you were. It's just one of those things that parents accidentally do without thinking ahead of any consequences. It wasn't serious.

You had a red chow that you bought for Connie when you were dating. You named him Leo. It seemed appropriate, since you were both Leo's under the zodiac sign. The dog looked like a lion. One day, your little niece came by to visit and she had on Minnie Mouse house shoes that squeaked when she walked. It drove Leo nuts. He went after April trying to bite her feet. Then a few weeks later, Leo nipped at Zack. That was it! Leo had to be put to sleep. It was one of the saddest decisions you had to make, but you couldn't allow anything like that to happen again. You had your priorities straight. That's what being a grown up is all about. You were in mourning for over two weeks.

I didn't think you were going to get past it.

Chapter 18

Your life started a downhill spiral. The world around you started to erode. Connie and you divorced. You lost your home to foreclosure. You lost your job after seventeen years of working for the county. You didn't know how you were going to put the pieces back together. You took odd jobs driving trucks but nothing lasted. You were a lost soul—just drifting—emotionally, financially and spiritually. You went through a very rough period of your life. There wasn't much that your Dad and I could do to help you, except provide a place for you to live.

As a mother, my help to you has often come at a high price. I, the enabler, have kept you from sleeping in the streets. In the long run it has taken away your own self-worth, dignity and the initiative to do something on your own. Hardships in life produce strong determined people like your Dad, who grew from adversity. Having it easy can weaken a person's character. Some will flounder from affluence and assistance. There's pride in working hard to accomplish something on your own.

Travis, you have had many ups and downs in your life. Your Dad and I have been with you for most of them. We know that you have been hurt from love but don't let that keep you from loving again. Love is the fuel that keeps us going. It fills us with grace and contentment. Let go of past resentments, guilt, hurts, and anger. Move on through faith. Find your glorious, innovative, imaginative spirit. Embrace the joyful things you used to do. And don't forget along the way to thank God for your many blessings.

Keep your lightheartedness of youth and expand your mature responsibilities. With your entrepreneurial skills you can invent something to improve on people's lives.

You have suffered from a lack of enthusiasm for life and a breakdown of hope. Set some goals and reach for the stars, and on your way, remember that happiness is contagious, expose everyone to it.

You will find your niche in life. If your job isn't satisfying, compensate by finding a hobby that you really enjoy. But whatever you do, do it well.

As for me, I was so fortunate to start out as a dancer. To get paid for something I loved to do was icing on the cake. I wish I had video tapes of my dancing years to share with you and Gregg. I also wish I had videos of your Dad lobbying and standing up for important issues. To see him setting a good example is important. When Red was a union leader and a legislator, he didn't always do the popular thing but he did the right thing. Your Dad would probably say to you, "if you don't stand firm on your beliefs—you don't stand at all."

Whenever I see the TV series of "Mash," I think of you. Travis, you remind me of Hawkeye, played by Alan Alda. It's the character's dry wit, wise cracks and jokes that are so typical of your personality. Maybe you should try acting or being a comedienne as a career.

You have excelled in making swing sets. You can do anything you put your mind to as long as you stay focused. Now, the next issue will be marketing your great ideas.

You have a special gift when it comes to understanding animals, especially dogs. I think of you as the dog whisperer.

Epilogue

Over a year ago, a strange thing happened. You seemed to grow up overnight. During the last year of your Dad's life, you became so responsible. Red was proud of you for putting in a lot of hours at work in order to make ends meet. I hope you know how much he appreciated you, and all your help around the house as things became more difficult for him to do. He's up in heaven smiling down on you so every now and then look upward and give him the thumbs up. I know he'll be giving the same sign back to you for doing such a fine job. I can hear him saying, "Keep up the good work, son. You have become the man I always knew you could be."

YOUR NAME

You got it from your father
It was all he had to give
So it's yours to use and cherish
For as long as you may live.
If you lose the watch he gave you
It can always be replaced
But a black mark on your name, son,
Can never be erased.
It was clean the day you took it
And a worthy name to bear
When he got it from his father,
There was no dishonor there.
So make sure you guard it wisely,
After all is said and done
You'll be glad the name is spotless
When you give it to your son.

Unknown

Books Written By Jorjan Jane

*STIMULUS OVERLOAD—A survival manual for those with Attention Deficit Disorder. If you can't concentrate or feel confused, it's not your fault. Your brain just had a short circuit. Learn how to focus and to cope so you can be productive.

*GREGORY—A story of love at first sight. His mother writes about her baby's humble beginnings. It tells of the trials and tribulations throughout their lives.

*TRAVIS—A story about a son's life, loves and pursuit of happiness. This book was written by his mom as a birthday gift. It's meant to remind him of his many talents.

*GRANDMA MOONED THE FOREST RANGER, nevertheless Memoirs of mom, a story of the difficulties of caring for an aging parent. The book was written as a coping mechanism, so you will find it has frustrating moments as well as humorous ones. This story is recommended for families and caretakers.

*UP BY THE BOOTSTRAPS—A story of a poor boy from Oklahoma who went from the farm to the oil fields, from a trucker to a pilot, from a cop to a labor leader, from a lobbyist to a senator. A book about his life, travels, and successes—all accomplished by honesty and hard work.